Budgeting Made Easy

The proven system for BREAKING the
paycheck-to-paycheck cycle, getting OUT of debt, and
LIVING THE LIFE you want

Budgeting Made Easy

Budgeting Made Easy

Gregg J. Boonstra

ColRy Publishing

Budgeting Made Easy

Budgeting Made Easy

Published by ColRy Publishing
12101 North MacArthur Boulevard
Office 256
Oklahoma City, Oklahoma 73162
A division of Vertical Vision, Inc.

All scripture quotations, unless otherwise indicated, are taken from the Holy Bible, New American Standard Version® Copyright © 1960, 1962, 1963, 1968, 1971, 1972, 1973, 1975, 1977, 1995 by The Lockman Foundation Used by permission." (www.Lockman.org)

Copyright © 2016 - 2019 by Gregg Boonstra

All rights reserved. No part of this book may be reproduced or transmitted in any form or by any means, electronic or mechanical, including photocopying and recording, or by any information storage and retrieval system, without permission in writing from the publisher.

Printed in the United States of America

Learn how to easily manage your finances and create financial security without changing your income.

A simple easy to use guide that will show you; how to manage your money, budget, and live debt free.

A simple easy to use guide that will help you:
- Budget
- Get out from under crushing debt
- Win with Money

Budgeting Made Easy

Table of Contents:

Table of Contents:	- 7 -
Introduction	- 9 -
Chapter 1: You Can't Believe Everything You Hear	- 11 -
Chapter 2: Making A Financial Plan That Works	- 27 -
Chapter 3: Dealing with Creditors	- 35 -
Chapter 4: The Role of Insurance	- 47 -
Chapter 5: Investments	- 61 -
Chapter 6: Now What	- 69 -
For More Budgeting Help and Encouragement	- 79 -
Contacting the Author	- 81 -
Forms	- 83 -
Monthly Income Worksheet	- 83 -
Budget Worksheet	- 87 -
Debt Pay Down Plan	- 97 -
Pro Rata Plan	- 101 -
Credit Dispute Letter	- 103 -

Budgeting Made Easy

Introduction

This book has been written as an easy to follow guide for those who would like to break the cycle of being broke, living paycheck to paycheck, or always feeling like they are one bill away from financial ruin.

Although the instructions may be easy, it will take discipline on your part. You may hit a few bumps along the way to financial success. It's okay, don't stop, keep going.

The road to financial success is much like the Little Train That Could, he had to just keep going even when times were tough. Follow the roadmap outlined in this book, modify for your needs, study more, and follow through.

Living without the constant worry of finances is well worth the time and effort. You will wonder why you lived with debt and financial trouble in the first place.

I have included many references to Bible passages in this book. Don't overlook them. Even if you do not believe in the Bible or God, the teachings in it are still very valuable and worth following.

As you read through this book, I highly suggest you have a pen in hand and write notes to yourself in the margins or circle and underline as you go through the book. These markings will help you go back through the book and find key information that is useful to you as you work on your financial journey.

Chapter 1: You Can't Believe Everything You Hear

Chapter 1: You Can't Believe Everything You Hear

Who taught you that borrowing money was a good idea? Are they here paying your bills now? Are they living your daily struggles? Let's look at some phrases that we have heard so many times that we think they are true (but they're not).

Loans are a part of life - This is a lie that has been spread over and over again. Yes, loans are a part of life for the average person, but the average person is buried in debt. Stop believing that loans need to be a part of your life.

Using credit is the responsible adult thing to do - Responsible adults do not spend more than they make. Responsible adults live on a budget. Responsible adults plan for emergencies and have money on hand for when emergencies happen.

It may be tight, but you'll be happier - This saying is often used when someone is looking at buying a house. I personally have never found it enjoyable to be tight, wondering if I will be able to pay my bills. If I lose my job or something breaks, I'll be beyond tight. I won't be able to pay the bills.

If you tell a lie often enough and loud enough, it eventually becomes accepted as truth. Marketing tells us that borrowing money is something everyone does. Marketing tells us we NEED to borrow money to be happy. Marketing tells us we need to get what we want when we want it. JUST DO IT. This is all a lie! You don't need to be in debt. You don't need to borrow to get what you want. You don't need to have everything and you certainly do not need to get it RIGHT NOW. Patience, you must practice patience and discipline.

Make sure that your character is free from the love of money, being content with what you

Chapter 1: You Can't Believe Everything You Hear

have; for He Himself has said, "I WILL NEVER DESERT YOU, NOR WILL I EVER FORSAKE YOU," Hebrews 13:5

You have fallen into the trap of not being content. You want what others have. You want those things that you think will make your life easier. You are willing to trade peace of mind and financial peace for instant gratification. This is not how God intends for you to live. God wants you to be content and rely on Him, not on debt or false ideas of what will make you happy.

No amount of marketing or lies changes the truth that borrowing today robs your future. What makes a successful marketing campaign is simple. To create a need where there wasn't a need before.

You need a safe shiny new car with easy payments.

> *You need a bigger and better TV, after all you deserve it.*
> *You need a new kitchen.*
> *You need a better lawn mower, it will make your grass greener.*
> *You need an ice cold soda.*
> *You need a candy bar, you deserve a break today, besides it's only a dollar.*
> *You need to buy two to get a deal.*

The average American sees over 3,000 commercial messages a day. Society, friends, and family are great at spreading all the lies that circulate around. They have bought into the mantra, they have failed to think for themselves and seek what is truly best.

> *You need to build your credit score.*
> *It's the responsible adult thing to do.*
> *Everyone borrows money. It may be tight, but you'll be happier.*
> *Car payments are a way of life.*

Chapter 1: You Can't Believe Everything You Hear

House payments are something everyone has for life.

Lies, lies, lies. Everyone of them is a lie.

The majority of people are broke. You need to refocus your vision. Stop looking at the immediate and look into the future. Money can be fun, but only when we use real money, money that doesn't come with a payment plan. When you're scared of the bills and the mailman, you're not having fun. Seven out of ten families are living paycheck to paycheck. That doesn't sound like fun. What happens when you have a couple of unpaid days off from work? What happens when you have an unexpected expense? Don't be part of the majority. Be wise. **Be different.**

<u>More money will not fix your problems.</u> When you mishandle money, more money will only amplify the problem. You'll incur larger debt payments, larger bills,

and make even more foolish spending decisions. Money problems are the number one cause of divorce. College students are racking up all kinds of debt. During the twelve month period ending in March 2013, over 1.17 million bankruptcies were filed.[i] Does this sound like everyone has it all together? Does this sound like the majority of people really know what they're doing with money? Are these the people you really want to be like?

You can try to avoid the facts. You blame others. You try to pacify your problems (usually by spending more). You try to look like you're doing great and you have it all together instead of dealing with reality. It's time to wake up. It's time to be an adult. It's time to be different. The key to your finances is YOU. The key to handling money wisely is YOUR behavior, not someone else's opinion. How do YOU handle YOUR money? You live in a world where the common practice

Chapter 1: You Can't Believe Everything You Hear

is to get what you want, when you want it. No waiting, no thinking. Just do it.

<u>*It's time to separate from the crowd.*</u> You will need discipline and you will need to set limits. **You'll find that limits don't constrain you, but quite the contrary, they'll set you free.** You need goals; you need to strive towards these goals. *What are your goals? Write them down.* A goal that you don't write down is quickly forgotten.

To live financially fit you will need to learn to be content. Seeing your progress with finances will be a huge motivator to being content. You'll find it easier to resist unnecessary purchases and be content with money in the bank and financial security.

In the Bible there are over 800 scripture passages about money. Why? Because it's important. God is fully aware of the pitfalls we will face and has said a great deal in His word to help you and guide you.

You need a plan, a purpose, and a roadmap to succeed with money. Write down, right now, the reasons why you want to succeed. Write it down now. We will work on the plan and roadmap in the coming pages.

There are five things you must understand.

First; *Debt robs your future!* Proverbs 22:7 teaches *The rich rules over the poor, And the borrower becomes the lender's slave.* When you are in debt, you are not free. You are enslaved to that debt. You do whatever you need to make sure you can make the payments. You stop taking vacations, you take jobs you don't want, you work so hard and have nothing to show for it.

Chapter 1: You Can't Believe Everything You Hear

Second; *You must spend less than you make!* This seems pretty obvious, but for some reason very few people follow this simple rule. You need to live like YOU, not the Joneses. Besides, the Joneses are broke and don't want you to know. Proverbs 21:20(KJV) states *There is treasure to be desired and oil in the dwelling of the wise; but a foolish man spendeth it up.* What's that? The wise man saves and the fool spends everything. It may seem hard at first, but you can live on less than you make. You can live without buying on debt.

Third; *You need a budget (one that works).* Get on a budget! You need a plan. You need to be responsible. You need to stick to your plan. You need to **WRITE** it down and **TRACK** it. You and your spouse must agree on it. A budget cannot be one sided. You must work together to develop a realistic budget that is within your income that you both agree on.

> *For which one of you, when he wants to build a tower, does not first sit down and calculate the cost to see if he has enough to complete it?* Luke 14:28

Fourth; *You must save and invest.* Yes, you can save. You need to have money on hand for emergencies. Cash is not the same as credit. Did you know that when you use credit you spend 12 – 18 percent more than you would if you were using cash? You must save and invest for your future.

Fifth; *Giving is important.* It is fun to give. Giving changes who you are. Oddly, giving is a natural part of life that will help your physical health and your mental health. It may not be easy to start. It will require discipline. If you keep going, it will become natural and you will find it hard to live any other way.

Chapter 1: You Can't Believe Everything You Hear

All discipline for the moment seems not to be joyful, but sorrowful; yet to those who have been trained by it, afterwards it yields the peaceful fruit of righteousness. Hebrews 12:11

Here are 10 practical steps you must take on this journey to your new financial future. Write these down. Post them on your refrigerator, write them on the bathroom mirror. Check them off as you complete them.

1. **Pray**. Prayer really works. If you messed up your finances, now is the time to let God know and ask for help moving forward. He loves you and wants to help you. Go ahead, talk to God. Stop trying to hide your problems. Let God know you need His help.
2. **Quit borrowing money**. You can't get out of a hole while you are still digging out the bottom. Instead of using the excuse of it was an

emergency, plan for them. You already know unexpected expenses will come up. Save money, build an emergency fund to pay for unexpected expenses.

3. **Plan how you spend.** Plan how you are spending and using the money that you have been entrusted with. Start a budget and stick to it. Budget less money than you make and use all "extra" money to pay down your debt.

4. **Save for emergencies.** Start by setting aside $1,000. Use this when emergencies happen. STOP using DEBT! Do you need help getting your $1,000? Have a yard sale, sell stuff.

5. **Debt Snowball.** Write down all your debts in order from smallest total balance to the largest balance. Any money that is "extra" pay towards your smallest balance.

6. **Save six months budget.** After you have paid off all your debt, save six months budget as your

Chapter 1: You Can't Believe Everything You Hear

new emergency fund. This will cover you during a time of job loss or major emergencies. Keep this money fluid; it is not to be tied up in an investment.

7. **Pay off your home.** Now that you have paid off all your debts and saved a six month emergency fund, it's time to get rid of the mortgage.

8. **Invest 15 percent of your income for retirement.** After your debt has been paid off, save for your later years. Take care of your retirement before funding a child's education.

9. **Fund education.** Now that you have enough income to pay your bills, and invest for your future, now is the time you can fund education. This happens only when you are debt free and are funding retirement. You can't retire on your child's education.

10. **Save and Give.** Now that you are 100 percent debt free, save money for those wants and find

ways to give to others and charity. People who give are happier.

You can't get ahead financially until you are free from debt. You currently spend about 50 percent of your income in debt payments. What could you do if you had no debt?

Start right now planning your budget. Use the budget worksheets from https://easybudget.money Write down what your true current spending is. We will work on how to write a realistic budget in the coming pages. Before you can write a realistic budget, you will need to know exactly how much you are really spending. Find your old bank statements and credit card statements. Go through them. Once you start writing down your real spending you'll probably be surprised and find patterns.

Chapter 1: You Can't Believe Everything You Hear

Don't continue to struggle. Make the choice today to improve your finances. Draw a line in the sand and take a stand making today the day that you will change. Change and change now to offer your family a better future, change to reduce stress and sleepless nights, change to honor God.

Budgeting Made Easy

Chapter 2: Making A Financial Plan That Works

Chapter 2: Making A Financial Plan That Works

Did you write down what your spending has been? What are a few things you learned while writing down your spending?

When you wrote down your spending you may have noticed that you were overspending by about 20 percent. You need to stop overspending. You need to quit borrowing money and spending money you don't have.

Go through your spending sheets and start making cuts. Be realistic. If you are spending $300 per month eating out, you can not cut that category down to zero. You'll need some money to eat out. If you make the cuts to drastic, the budget won't work. You'll think it's too hard and quit. Your goal as you go through is to make the total at least 5 percent less than your take home pay. You may need to go through several times. It may take a couple of days.

What if you have an income that varies? Is it impossible to budget? No, it is not impossible. The way you handle this is pretty simple. I suggest you set up a bank account to deposit all your income into. Figure out what your regular take home pay is. Then on payday, withdraw from that account your "regular" income and deposit it into your regular checking account. Extra money in that account will accumulate and cover the gap for when you have a low income. By doing this, you have forced yourself to live on a regular amount of money every pay day. If the account balance builds too much, use some of the "extra" money to pay down debt.

Remember that while writing your budget, it is important to give. At first while you are working on

Chapter 2: Making A Financial Plan That Works

getting out of debt, the amount you give may be small. That's okay. As you become better at managing the money entrusted to you, you will have more money available to give.

All a budget really is; it is a plan for how you will spend your money. The key to your finances is YOUR behavior, how well you follow YOUR plan. You will need discipline to stick to the plan. You need goals. Without goals you have no target to shoot for. You will have no reason to continue budgeting when times are hard. Goals will be your constant reminder and reason for staying on track. You must write your goals down. You should post your goals where you will regularly see them. You need to learn how to be content with what you have, and be patient while saving for the things you would like.

Budgeting Made Easy

A budget is no good if you don't follow it. You must know exactly how much money you take home after taxes and all deductions. You must track every single expense. You must know how much money you spent from each budget category. You must know how much money you have available in your budget category before you spend any money. If for some reason you must overspend a category, you will need to adjust your budget. You may not adjust your budget by raising the total budget. You will need to reduce from one category the amount you want to add to another. Your budget will not be right the first time. That's okay. You need to start somewhere. As you notice areas where your budget is incorrect you will need to adjust.

While you are in debt, you will budget to make only minimum payments on all of your debts. Nothing more. I know that this may sound crazy, but trust me it works. Any extra money you have will be paid to the debt with

Chapter 2: Making A Financial Plan That Works

the smallest total balance. Once the smallest debt is paid off, you will then take the minimum payment you were paying on that debt and add it to the amount you are paying towards the next debt on the list. Once again, any extra money you receive/find will be used to pay towards the lowest balance debt currently on the list. By following this method you will quickly whittle away at your debts giving you regular "wins" as you eliminate one debt after another. While paying down debt; pause saving for retirement. The amount of interest that you are paying to debt is higher than any interest you are earning on your retirement account. It is to your advantage to retire your debt first. Also, while you are in debt; pause saving for education expenses.

Here are some practical things you can do to help you stay on budget.

Shop with a list. Make a list before you go shopping. If it isn't on the list, you don't buy it.

Plan your groceries on a calendar. Print out a blank calendar. For every day of the month fill in what meals you plan to eat. You can then buy the groceries you need according to the plan. By doing this, you will reduce the over repetitive I don't know what to eat so we'll just make the same thing we always do problem. You will also eliminate the I don't know what to eat so we'll just go out for dinner problem.

Grocery shop once a month. Once you are shopping with a list and planning your meals on a calendar, it will be easy to grocery shop once a month. Think of the time you will save. In addition to saving time, people who shop once per month save about 25 percent on their grocery category because they aren't buying extras. You may need to do some stops at the store for milk, bread, and produce, but when you do, you simply pick up only the things on your list and only what you cannot buy once per month.

Chapter 2: Making A Financial Plan That Works

Track every penny spent. Every penny matters. Make sure you write it down every time you spend money. Make sure you write it down in the correct budget category. Make sure you are not overspending a category, not even by a penny.

Meet with your spouse regularly to check in on your budget and to make adjustments. The two of you must work together and know how you are doing in order to stay on track.

ACCOUNTABILITY. Remember, the key to your finances is YOUR behavior, not your knowledge, not your neighbors spending, not anything other than YOU and how YOU are behaving with YOUR money. It is wise to find someone you trust who will check in with you and ask you the tough questions. Are you spending your money wisely? Are you staying on budget?

By knowing that someone is going to be checking up on you, you are more likely to stay on track.

We live in a world where you get what you want, when you want it. No waiting, no thinking, just do it. You need to change your way of thinking and learn to be content.

You need a plan, a purpose, and a roadmap to get there.

If you haven't started yet, get started now. Write down your goals. Write down the 10 steps we will follow. Write down your budget. You can find a budget worksheet at https://easybudget.money Feel free to copy it. Make a commitment to God that you are going to honor Him by properly managing the money He entrusted to your care.

Chapter 3: Dealing with Creditors

Now the serpent was more crafty than any beast of the field which the Lord God had made. And he said to the woman, "Indeed, has God said, 'You shall not eat from [a]any tree of the garden'?" The woman said to the serpent, "From the fruit of the trees of the garden we may eat; but from the fruit of the tree which is in the middle of the garden, God has said, 'You shall not eat from it or touch it, or you will die.'" The serpent said to the woman, "You surely will not die! For God knows that in the day you eat from it your eyes will be opened, and you will be like God, knowing good and evil." When the woman saw that the tree was good for food, and that it was a delight to the eyes, and that the tree was

> *desirable to make one wise, she took from its fruit and ate; and she gave also to her husband with her, and he ate.* Genesis 3:1-6

They had everything. Satan tempted them by telling them that they could have even more if they ate of the forbidden fruit. It's the same today. Satan tells you that you can have more, and not only can you have more but you deserve it. You are being restricted from the good things if you don't get it now. Just use debt and easy payments and you will have everything you ever wanted.

Follow the trappings of easy credit and "easy" payments and you will soon learn that those wonderful promises really aren't so wonderful. Those debt payments become your slave master keeping you from being truly free.

Chapter 3: Dealing with Creditors

Do you know how your credit score is calculated? Credit scores are calculated based on the debt load you carry. It's not based on your income, or your honesty. FICO stands for Fair Isaac Corporation. Your credit score is a made up number by a company that profits from making up credit score numbers. Your score is based on:

- 35% Your debt history
- 30% Your debt levels
- 15% Length of credit
- 10% Type of debt
- 10% New debt

If your debts are too high or if your debts are too low your score will be lowered. Your FICO score has nothing to do with the amount of money you have or the amount of money you make. The credit score is simply a number that shows how much you love being in debt. You do not need a credit score to obtain a mortgage. There are lenders who base their loans on income and true verifiable information, not on debt. It's an I like to have things now and not wait until I can afford them score.

Let's talk about your credit reports. On your credit report, chapter 7 bankruptcies are removed after 10 years, other debt information is removed after 7 years.

        79% of credit reports contain mistakes

        25% contain serious errors resulting in the denial of credit

        30% list accounts as open that have been closed

        22% list the same mortgage twice

You should check your credit report. Not because you should go into debt, but because your credit report is used for many more things than receiving credit. You can check your credit report from the three major credit reporting agencies (Experian, Equifax, TransUnion) for free annually by going to

Chapter 3: Dealing with Creditors

www.annualcreditreport.com You do not need to pay and you do not need your credit score or any other option that has a fee.

When you find inaccurate information on your credit report you can have it removed by writing a letter to the agency reporting the inaccurate information. Include in the letter the account number, creditor name, and balances that inaccurate. Most of the credit bureaus have a website that you can use to notify them of inaccurate information instead of sending them a letter. Credit bureaus must remove the inaccurate information within 30 days of notification.

If you have been the victim of identity theft, place a fraud victim alert with each of the three major credit reporting agencies (Experian, Equifax, TransUnion). A fraud victim alert will stay active for 90 days unless you make it permanent by getting a police report. You owe

NOTHING on fraudulent charges and you should pay NOTHING on fraudulent charges. If you receive phone calls or letters demanding payment for fraudulent charges you simply notify them that they are fraud and you owe nothing. You should also notify the fraud division at each creditor reporting outstanding fraudulent debts.

Collection Practices:
Maybe you've been contacted by a collection agency. Maybe you know someone else who has and you can help them.

The best way to pay a debt is with a plan. If you cannot afford to pay minimum payments on all of your debts you should develop a Pro Rata plan. In a pro rata plan you add up all the debts and figure out the percentage of debt that you owe to each creditor. You then figure out how much money you have available to pay towards debt. Each creditor receives a percentage

Chapter 3: Dealing with Creditors

of the money you have available based on the percentage of debt you have with them. You can use the form at https://easybudget.money to help you figure out your pro rata plan.

Pro Rata Fair Share Plan

Debt Payment Money: $ __200__   Total Debt Payments: __2,000__

Debt:	Total Due:	Total Debt Payments: (see above)	Percent of Debt:	Debt Payment Money	Amount I Can Pay Now:
Sears	100 /	2,000	= 5% (.05) x	200	= $10
Bank of America	200 /	2,000	= 10% (.10) x	200	= $20
Discover	200 /	2,000	= 10% (.10) x	200	= $20
Amex	300 /	2,000	= 15% (.15) x	200	= $30
Home Depot	1,200 /	2,000	= 60% (.60) x	200	= $120
	/		=	x	=
	/		=	x	=

Once you have your pro rata plan, you may tell your creditors that you cannot afford to pay their minimums, but you have developed a pro rata plan. You can send them a copy of your plan.

A debt collector's job is to get money. They are not your friend. A debt collector does not care about you. They may listen to you and pretend to care, but they don't. The only reason that they listen is to find a way to twist what you say and find a way to convince you to pay them. The average debt collector averages 20 calls per hour. It is a low paying job with 85% turnover. Do not be intimidated by a debt collector.

A debt collector is trained to invoke strong emotion (bait and switch). They keep detailed records on what works when they are speaking with you. If they can get you emotional (angry, crying, or upset) they can then use your emotions to make you pay.

A debt collector is not the person you borrowed from. Many collectors will talk as if you borrowed the money from them and owe them personally. Don't let them make you believe that you owe them personally. It is just part of their game of playing with your emotions.

Chapter 3: Dealing with Creditors

If you decide to settle with a debt collector get the deal in writing first. Do not make any kind of payment on a deal without a written agreement. They are very well known for taking your money and then claiming they never made the agreement. Never allow a collector access to your account. When making payments always do it with a check or some form of payment that you send, not one where they take the money from your account.

Before paying your debts, you need to take care of your necessities. Your necessities are first, debt comes after you pay for food, shelter (mortgage or rent), basic utilities (phone, electric, heat), and transportation. If you take care of your necessities first you will be in a much better mental and physical condition to deal with your creditors and earn the money you need to pay them.

The Federal Fair Debt Collection Practices Act states that a collector may only contact you between the hours of 8:00am and 9:00 pm your time. If they call you outside of this time, they are breaking the law. You may also demand that they stop calling you at work. You can also demand that they stop calling you completely, but this is not a good idea. Once all communication is cut off they are more likely to sue you.

Make debt collectors follow your rules. This will help you be better prepared to speak with them. Agree to speak with them twice a month. Tell them that they may call you on something like the 1st and the 15th of every month. A first they won't listen. When they do call outside of the parameters that you set, kindly remind them that you said you would speak with them on the 1st and 15th. Today is neither the 1st or 15th so you will not be speaking with them today. If they would like to speak with you they must call back on at the correct time.

Chapter 3: Dealing with Creditors

Then simply hang up the phone. Do not argue, do not yell, try not to show emotion.

Debt collectors may not seize your accounts or garnish your wages without court approval. They may call and threaten all kinds of things, but if a judge has not approved it and provided a written judgment, then the collector is lying. To garnish your wages or take money from your bank they must sue you, win the lawsuit, receive a judgment, wait 30 days and then execute on the judgment. If they do sue you, you will be served papers by the local sheriff's office. You will typically be served at least 10 days prior to a court date. Even after a judgment, you can settle with a creditor. After a judgment you can also file a slow pay motion or a "pauper's oath" with the court. A slow pay is granted when you can show the judge your budget and prove you do not currently have enough income to pay the debt. The debt will not be erased, but the judge will allow you to pay back small portions using your pro rata plan.

If a creditor is breaking the law, I recommend you record the phone calls. When a creditor calls, you tell them your name, the time, and that you are recording the call, then let them talk. If they broke the law, you can call back and ask for their legal department. Play the recording for them and they will most likely offer you a very good deal to settle right away. If they do not respond you can file a lawsuit against them. They will avoid being sued at all costs because judges are very quick to revoke a debt collectors license to do business.

Chapter 4: The Role of Insurance

How are you doing with your financial plan? If you haven't written your budget yet, stop now and go do it. You cannot get ahead until you start to write down your plan and follow it.

> *Thus says the LORD, "Let not a wise man boast of his wisdom, and let not the mighty man boast of his might, let not a rich man boast of his riches;* [24] *but let him who boasts boast of this, that he understands and knows Me, that I am the LORD who exercises loving kindness, justice and righteousness on earth; for I delight in these things," declares the LORD.* Jeremiah 9:23-24

Insurance is a financial planning tool. It is a planning tool, not a savings tool or a financial wealth tool. The purpose of insurance is to transfer risk. By purchasing insurance, you transfer some of the risk of an insured event to the insurance company. If you have a significant loss or a catastrophe could you afford it?

An example would be, when I buy collision insurance or "full coverage" insurance on my car, I am asking the insurance company to take the risk of paying for the damage to my car if it is involved in an accident. Without collision insurance, when I'm involved in an accident, I am required to pay for the repairs to my own car. However, when I do have collision insurance, the insurance company is required to pay for the damage to my car. If I have an older car that isn't worth much, should I have collision insurance? Well, the answer comes in the form of a question. If I have an accident, can I afford to repair my car or replace it? If I cannot afford the repairs to my car, it may be wise for me to pay

Chapter 4: The Role of Insurance

for insurance so that when I do have an accident, the insurance company is responsible for the costs.

This example could be applied to all forms of insurance. If a loss happens can I afford it? Do I have the money I need to cover the loss? If the answer is no, then it may be wise to purchase insurance to cover such a loss. Many insurance agents will tell you that insurance is a great savings tool. Don't buy into this lie. Insurance is not a savings tool or a wealth building tool. Insurance is a risk transfer tool. It should only be used to protect you from a loss that you cannot afford.

Insurances worth considering are:

Homeowners or Renters Insurance. If you have a full emergency fund, you can raise your deductibles to lower your premiums. Remember, insurance is to cover a loss you cannot afford. If you have an emergency fund, you can afford a small loss up to the amount of emergency money you have. With a $1,000 emergency fund, you can afford to lose up to $1,000. If a loss happens, you pay the $1,000 deductible and let the insurance company cover the rest.

You should carry adequate liability insurance. We live in a society where people sue very quickly and for very frivolous reasons. The liability insurance you carry should be adequate to cover "dumb" lawsuits. Say if a person came to your door and tripped on your step. They can sue you and win. Your insurance should cover "dumb" losses like this.

Homeowners insurance should be "Guaranteed Replacement Cost". Most policies are "extended replacement cost" meaning they'll add about 10% to what your policy is written for. But if your house has gained in value you want to make sure your policy will cover it. That is why you choose "Guaranteed Replacement Cost". If my house has gained in value from $100,000 to $150,000, I want the insurance company to be responsible for replacing the total value of $150,000 should my house be destroyed.

Umbrella. Umbrella policies are good to protect your assets. In our lawsuit happy society, if you have something of value and are sued, you could be required to liquate everything you have to pay for the lawsuit. With an umbrella policy, the insurance may be able to cover a loss such as a lawsuit against you. Umbrella policies cover you and protect your assets. These policies are not protecting a specific item such as a house or car.

Auto Insurance. If you have a car, you must have auto insurance. Basic auto insurance pays for damages that you cause to others. If you have an accident and damage someone else's property/car, the insurance company will pay to repair the other person's property/car. It is never wise to drive if you do not have auto insurance.

What about collision insurance? You need to consider the risk and the breakeven point. If you save $100 per year by cancelling collision, how long must you have no accidents or losses to make the savings worthwhile. Assume you have a small accident every ten years. Being small, the cost to repair your car is only $2,000. If you opted to keep your collision insurance, over ten years you would have paid $1,000 in premiums. The insurance company is now required to pay the $2,000 to repair your car. You have actually ended up ahead because the cost of the repair is more than the premiums you have paid. Another reason to keep collision is because you cannot afford the loss. If you are not in a position to pay for repairs to your car if you have an accident, it is wise to have insurance that will pay for the repairs.

Health Insurance. Well, simply we all get sick. You will use health insurance. The bigger question is how much. If you are generally healthy and rarely need medical care, then you may want a policy with higher deductibles/co-pays. If you choose higher deductibles/co-pays, make sure you place money aside to pay the deductibles when you need to. When you are cutting insurance premiums, increase the out of pocket expense such as co-pays, but never decrease the maximum payout. You want your insurance to cover all expenses if you have a major illness. If you develop an aggressive cancer or illness, the medical cost could be extremely expensive. By having no maximum payout, the insurance company is responsible for paying all of the medical costs above your co-pay. If you have a maximum payout of $50,000, this most likely will not even cover a minor surgery, and defiantly will not cover a major illness. Medical costs are extremely high, make sure you are covered.

An HSA or FSA may be a great way to help you with medical costs. They are simply savings accounts that are not taxed. The money in these accounts can only be used to pay for medical costs. HSA, is a "Health Savings Account". HSA's can be setup with your local bank. You may want to consider putting in that account the amount of money you will need to cover all of your co-pays. When you deposit money into the account, it is considered pre-tax money. An FSA is a "Flexible Spending Account". An FSA is setup with your employer. Not every employer participates in FSA's. Like a savings account, you deposit pre-tax money into the account to use for paying your out of pocket medical expenses. You must keep in mind however that all the money in an FSA must be spent every year or you lose the money. Do not over fund an FSA.

Disability Insurance. Disability insurance is designed to replace income lost due to a short term or permanent disability. The average person has a 33% chance of becoming disabled at some point in your life. Your risk is actually quite high. When buying disability insurance, it is important to know that not all disability insurance is the same. You want to purchase insurance that pays if you cannot perform the job that you were educated or trained to do. This is called "Occupational Insurance". Beware also of policies that cover less than five years. If you cannot work for more than five years, you want to be covered. Just because my insurance ran out, it doesn't mean that my life expenses such as rent, food, and electric stop. No, I want insurance that will continue to pay, so that I can continue to pay my bills.

Long Term Care Insurance. It is recommended to purchase this insurance at age 60. This insurance will pay for nursing homes, assisted living, and in-home care. Taking care of aging parents is a huge financial burden facing a lot of people today. This insurance will help to make sure that you do not place that burden on your family. It may also be wise for you to talk with your parents about their long-term care. If they need care, are you going to be able to afford it? Do they have the finances to pay for it? 69% of people over the age of 65 will require long term care at some point during their life. Contrary to popular belief, someone needing long term care cannot just transfer their assets and use Medicaid to pay for everything.

Identity Theft Protection. Identity theft is on the rise. Access to your personal information is way too easy. Statistics are showing that it is highly likely that you will be the victim of some form of identity theft. When

Chapter 4: The Role of Insurance

looking at identity theft protection, you should look for a policy that offers "restoration services" and one that offers you a person who is responsible for cleaning things up when your identity is stolen. Many "Identity Theft" policies only offer monitoring. Monitoring will do nothing to restore your identity after it has been stolen. It can only tell you that it has been stolen. Once your identity has been stolen the costs can be very high and time involved to restore it can be hundreds of hours of work.

Life Insurance. Life insurance is to replace income due to death. I recommend only Term life insurance. In most cases, I recommend that you do not buy "Whole Life", "Cash Value", or "Permanent" plans. These plans have a savings plan built in. As we discussed earlier, insurance is not a savings plan or wealth building tool. It is a financial planning tool that should be used to protect you. The reason I recommend term life insurance is because if you continue to work your financial plan, your needs will change in the next 10 and 20 years. Your kids will be grown and gone, the mortgage will be paid off, you will have no more debt, and you will have a retirement account already well funded. You may not even need life insurance once you have reached the end of your term policy.

Buy a life insurance policy valued at ten times your income. This is very valuable to a family that is dependent on your paycheck. If you die, what will your family do to earn money? How will your family continue to pay the bills? With a proper life insurance policy in place, the payout of the policy can be invested, and your family can use the interest of the investments to replace your income.

Don't forget the value of a stay at home spouse. Even though your spouse doesn't bring money into the family,

Chapter 4: The Role of Insurance

if they die what will happen? The hard part is trying to understand what the value of those services are. If someone is a stay at home spouse, you will need to estimate how much it will cost to pay someone to do what they do. You then buy a term life insurance policy valued at ten times your estimate. If a person who stays home dies, the household duties of that person must be continued. If that person is insured, the payout from the policy can be invested and the interest from the investment can be used to pay for other people to do the household functions.

Right now, set a date that you will have your insurances in place by. Make it within the next month. Review your existing policies this week and start shopping for insurance. Within one month, have all the insurance that you need to protect you when life happens. What is that date? Write it down now.

I will have my insurance in place by:
_____

Chapter 5: Investments

> *All discipline for the moment seems not to be joyful, but sorrowful; yet to those who have been trained by it, afterwards it yields the peaceful fruit of righteousness.* Hebrews 12:11

Over the past couple of chapters, we have been talking about being disciplined. We have talked about the need to wait for things until you can afford them. We talked about how you can't always get everything you want right away. We don't always know why we need to wait. We don't always know why God doesn't just give us everything we want. We do know however that God loves us and in Hebrews 12:11 He tells us that discipline does not always seem joyful, but by being disciplined, we will learn and grow from it. We ask why, why, why, but God says be patient.

When investing, you must be disciplined and not greedy. You must be disciplined and willing to wait. When looking at your returns, it's important to look at the percentages, not the dollars or "points". Let's look at Sam and Kelly. Sam invested $100 and Kelly invested $1,000. At the end of their first month investing, they both earned $50. Who had better investments? Whose investments grew more. They both earned the same amount of money, but Sam made better investments. Sam earned a 50% return, while Kelly earned only a 5% return.

When investing, I highly suggest using a brokerage firm like Charles Schwab and not investing at a bank or a place that only lets you invest in their investment products. At a place like Charles Schwab you can invest in anything you choose. They do offer their own mutual

Chapter 5: Investments

funds, but you are also free to invest in any investment available on the market. Also, do not invest in anything you do not understand, even if you are using a broker or a financial guru. It is important that you understand your investments. Do not let your broker be your only teacher. Go to the library, read, take a class or two. Whatever you must do, do it. But never invest in something that you do not understand.

Just because you know someone, that doesn't mean that they are good at investing. People at church often invest with others from church. Even if they tell you they know a lot, or sound really good, they may not be. Do homework and learn about others. Compare your options and make a wise decision about how you will invest.

It's very important to diversify. This means to spread your investment across several different options. The reason you do this is because if your investment loses, you won't lose everything, you will only lose what you invested in that one investment. All your other investments are still in place, you only lost that one.

Here are some basic terms that you should know when investing:

> Large Cap – Big companies
> Mid Cap– Midsize companies
> Small Cap – Small companies
> Blue chips – Blue chips are the stocks of nationally known companies whose value and dividends are reliable
> Stocks – Stocks are part ownership in a company
> Bonds – Bonds are a loan to someone, frequently a government
> Commodities (Futures) – Commodities are future products such as corn, wheat, oil that has not yet been harvested.

Chapter 5: Investments

Mutual Funds – Mutual funds are investments that buy and sell other investments like stocks. These are where I suggest you invest.

12b-1 Fee – This is a fee that a fund charges for marketing

Alpha – Alpha shows a funds risk adjusted performance against its index. A positive alpha number means that the fund has outperformed the index.

Annual Turnover – The amount the funds' assets have changed over a one-year period

Beta – Beta shows how volatile (risky) a fund is compared to its index

Manager – The manager is the person who oversees the fund

Load – This is like a commission that you pay to the fund

NAV (Net Asset Value) – The total of everything owned by the fund

Manager Tenure – The length of time that the current manager has managed the fund.

How do you pick a fund to invest in? Start by looking at the return over time (Performance). Has the fund consistently had a good return? Look at the fees. Is it expensive to buy or sell the fund? What is the Morningstar rating? There are so many funds available that I suggest you only buy ones that are rated four or

Chapter 5: Investments

five stars. Compare the historic risk and the historic return. Look for funds that have a low risk but a high return. Most investment firms offer all of this information for free on their websites.

Once you decide to buy investments, track their percentage progress weekly. Selling an investment that is a loser is often better than waiting for it to turn around. All the time that you wait for an investment to turn around, you could have invested the money in something that was performing well.

Set your thresholds and stick to them. This is where discipline is very important. Set a threshold for how much you would like to gain from an investment. When it reaches your goal, sell it. Set a threshold for how much it can lose. When it loses too much, sell it. Never forget to diversify.

These are some of the basic guidelines and some basic information about investing. You must choose your investments based on your own knowledge and research. Remember to never invest in anything until you understand what you are investing in.

Chapter 6: Now What

Now that you are budgeting and living with-in your means, the next question is usually how do I buy those big things. How do I buy furniture, cars, appliances? The answer is quite simple. You budget for them. Each month you put money into a category for an item you want to buy. Just like you budget every month for groceries, you budget every month for a car. Assume that you want to buy a used car in two years. You estimate that you will want to spend about $10,000 for that car. Now it's pretty simple. Two years is 24 months. 10,000 divided by 24 is 416.67. Now you know that to buy a $10,000 car in two years, you will need to budget $416.67 every month for that car. At the end of the two years you will have enough cash to pay for the car.

What if you need it now? Buy something smaller and more modest that will get you by until you can afford bigger and better. If you buy a cheaper car today, you can continue to save for a more expensive car later. The cheaper car will get you by until you have cash on hand to pay for the better car.

> *The rich rules over the poor, And the borrower becomes the lender's slave.*
>
> Proverbs 22:7

Once you take a loan. You become a slave to the lender. Not sometimes, but all the time. You are required to do whatever it takes to make those payments. If you didn't earn enough, if you lost your job, if you had some unexpected bills, it doesn't matter. The lender wants their money. You are enslaved to them first. You are required to pay them. Don't become a slave. Do not borrow money.

Chapter 6: Now What

Anytime we see the Bible talk about debt, it's bad. Not once in the Bible do we see a reference to debt and it turns out to be okay. The Bible consistently talks about how destructive debt can be. God will bless you and take care of you when you do things His way.

We need to filter our financial decisions through the examples and instructions that God laid out in His word, the Bible. I call this using our Biblical glasses. We should always filter what we do while looking at it through our Biblical glasses. God didn't say to do it the way everyone else is doing it. God asks that we do it His way, and when we follow God's way, it will work. It doesn't always make sense to us. We have our regular human logic and our regular wants. When we look at things from a Biblical perspective however, we see time and time again how things didn't make logical sense, but when God's word was followed it all worked out wonderful, but when God's word was not followed, things fell apart. One classic example is when God freed the Israelites from Egypt. He gave them specific instructions on how they should prepare to be freed. The Israelites obeyed, and Pharaoh set them free. God guided the Israelites to the land he wanted to give them. Again, He gave them instructions to take over the promised land. The Israelites decided to check for themselves if God's plan made sense. They sent 12 spies into the land to scope it out and report back. Ten spies said that they could not take the land and two, Joshua and Caleb said they should obey God and take over the land. The people decided to follow human logic and do things their way. What happened next is that the Israelites wondered homeless for 40 years. After the 40 years, God once again gave them instructions on how to take over the promised land. This time, even though the instructions didn't make logical sense, they obeyed God. Guess what, the plan worked. They were given

Chapter 6: Now What

the land when they obeyed God's way. To read the story, go to Numbers 13 in your Bible.

> *For this reason I bow my knees before the Father, from whom every family in heaven and on earth derives its name, that He would grant you, according to the riches of His glory, to be strengthened with power through His Spirit in the inner man, so that Christ may dwell in your hearts through faith; and that you, being rooted and grounded in love, may be able to comprehend with all the saints what is the breadth and length and height and depth, and to know the love of Christ which surpasses knowledge, that you may be filled up to all the fullness of God.*
>
> *Now to Him who is able to do far more abundantly beyond all that we ask or think, according to the power that works within us, to*

> *Him be the glory in the church and in Christ*
> *Jesus to all generations forever and ever. Amen.*
> Ephesians 3:14-21

God is able to far more than we realize. We need to trust Him to do abundantly in us. However, for God to do abundant things through us, we must trust, and follow His ways and His instructions.

God trusted you to care for His money. If God entrusted His money to you, don't you think you should handle it according to His instructions? The devil doesn't want you to follow God's ways. The devil is sneaky and misleading. You MUST make sure you use Biblical glasses. God does not do anything contrary to His word. The devil tries to trick you by making things seem mostly Biblical, or seem like a good way of doing things, but if it doesn't follow Biblical example exactly, then it's not from God.

Many times, we say that we trust God, but as soon as a problem arises, we try to solve it our way. Sometimes, we just need to be patient. Sometimes we just need to seek God. We are too quick to do it our way and look for the answer we want.

> *for we walk by faith, not by sight*
> 2 Corinthians 5:7

We know the verse so well. We even quote it "we walk by faith…". However, we seem to want to solve the world's problems, our problems on our own instead of relying on the One who created the world and promised to care for you.

Be of sober spirit, be on the alert. Your adversary, the devil, prowls around like a roaring lion, seeking someone to devour.
I Peter 5:8

Render to all what is due them: tax to whom tax is due; custom to whom custom; fear to whom fear; honor to whom honor. Owe nothing to anyone except to love one another; for he who loves his neighbor has fulfilled the law. For this, "YOU SHALL NOT COMMIT ADULTERY, YOU SHALL NOT MURDER, YOU SHALL NOT STEAL, YOU SHALL NOT COVET," and if there is any other commandment, it is summed up in this saying, "YOU SHALL LOVE YOUR NEIGHBOR AS YOURSELF." Love does no wrong to a neighbor; therefore love is

Chapter 6: Now What

the fulfillment of the law. Do this, knowing the time, that it is already the hour for you to awaken from sleep; for now salvation is nearer to us than when we believed. The night is almost gone, and the day is near. Therefore let us lay aside the deeds of darkness and put on the armor of light. Let us behave properly as in the day, not in carousing and drunkenness, not in sexual promiscuity and sensuality, not in strife and jealousy. But put on the Lord Jesus Christ, and make no provision for the flesh in regard to its lusts.

Romans 13:7-14

Make a commitment TODAY to handle finances the way God wants them handled.

Budgeting Made Easy

For More Budgeting Help and Encouragement

You can follow a simple online course developed to help guide you through the principles in this book. To view the online course, go to: https://easybudget.money

In addition to the online course, there are many other great resources at https://easybudget.money including:
- Budget Forms
- Pro Rata Forms for working with creditors
- Simple Net Worth Statements
- Secret Private Facebook Group for help and encouragement from others just like you
- Helpful tips
- Encouragement

Budgeting Made Easy

Contacting the Author

Gregg travels speaking to groups and orginazations about personal finance. If you would like to schedule Gregg to speak to your group, you may contact him at: gregg.boonstra@easybudget.money

Gregg also works with some clients directly one on one. This is done in person and via online video conferencing. If you would like to know more about working directly with Gregg on your personal finances, you may contact him by emailing: gregg.boonstra@easybudget.money

You can also write to Gregg at:
Gregg Boonstra
c/o ColRy Publishing a division of Vertical Vision
12101 N. MacArthur Blvd.
Office 256
Oklahoma City, Oklahoma 73162

Budgeting Made Easy

Forms

All of these forms can be downloaded at: https://easybudget.money

Monthly Income Worksheet:

Start by writing the month name in the blank "Income for the Month of"

Write in the amount of your monthly budget in the blank "My Budget for the Month is"

Every time you receive income, write it down on one of the lines. Include the date, a short description of what the income is, and the amount you received.

Add all your income lines together and write the total amount in the blank "Total Income"

Write the amount you budgeted in the blank "Budgeted Amount"

Subtract the "Budget Amount" from the "Total Income" and write the total in "Amount for Debt Snowball"

If the amount you write in "Amount for Debt Snowball" is a negative number, you did not make enough money to cover the amount you budgeted. You have overspent and will need to adjust your spending next month so you do not continue to overspend.

If the amount is not a negative number, Congratulations. This is the amount of "extra" money you made. Use this "extra" money to pay down debt or if you are out of debt, use it towards a financial goal.

Forms

Example:

Monthly Income Worksheet:

Income for the Month of: _July 2010_   My Budget for this Month is: $ _1,500.00_
                (Month Name)

Date:	Description of Income Source:	Amount:
7/2/2010	Work Paycheck (Factory)	751.23
7/10/2010	Second Job Paycheck (Pizza Shop)	84.99
7/16/2010	Work Paycheck (Factory)	701.54
7/19/2010	Garage Sale	212.85

             Total Income: _1750.61_ add all income amounts and
                                        write the amount here

         - Budgeted Amount: $ 1,500.00

     = Amount for Debt Snowball: _250.61_ Budgeted Amount – Total Income
                                           = The amount to write here

Budgeting Made Easy

There is hope.

Monthly Income Worksheet:

Income for the Month of: _____   My Budget for this Month is: _____
(Month Name)

Date:	Description of Income Source:	Amount:
_____	_____	_____
_____	_____	_____
_____	_____	_____
_____	_____	_____
_____	_____	_____
_____	_____	_____
_____	_____	_____
_____	_____	_____
_____	_____	_____
_____	_____	_____
_____	_____	_____
_____	_____	_____
_____	_____	_____
_____	_____	_____
_____	_____	_____
_____	_____	_____

Total Income: _____   add all income amounts and write the amount here

- Budgeted Amount: _____

= Amount for Debt Snowball: _____   Budgeted Amount – Total Income = The amount to write here

If the Amount for Debt Snowball is a negative number, than you did not make enough money this month.

web: www.verticalvisionokla.com

12101 North MacArthur Blvd Box 256
Oklahoma City, Oklahoma 73162

Budget Worksheet Instructions:

On the first page (income) write in the amount of net income per month on the amount line. Write a description of the payment on the description/frequency line.

To calculate monthly amounts:
- For weekly payments, multiply the amount by 52. Divide the answer by 12.
- For twice monthly payments multiply the amount by 2.
- For every other week payments multiply the amount by 26. Divide the answer by 12.

Add up all the amounts and place the answer in the Total Monthly Income blank. This is the total amount of money you have available to spend every month.

Multiply the Total Monthly Income by 12 and place the answer in the Total Annual Income. This is the total amount of spendable income you have available for the whole year.

I suggest you use pencil for the next section:
On the following pages (expenses) write in the total amount you spend per month for each item listed. If you have items not listed, use the other blank for the category it belongs in (make sure to write in what it is next to the word other).

Add up all the amounts and place the answer in the Total Monthly Expenses blank. This is the amount of money you spend every month.

Next place the total amount of monthly income from the first page in the blank for Total Monthly Income. Place the total monthly expenses from the expense section (just above this section) in the Total Monthly Expenses blank. Subtract Total Monthly Expenses from Total Monthly Income; write the answer in the Difference blank. If the amount in difference is a negative number, then you are overspending by this amount. You need to adjust your monthly expenses so that you are no longer overspending.

If the amount in difference is a positive number, congratulations, you are spending less than you make. This money should be used to build an emergency fund, pay down debt, and save for future goals.

Budgeting Made Easy

Vertical Vision

There is hope.

Budget Worksheet

Income	Amount	Description/Frequency
Job 1 _____	_____	_____
Job 2 _____	_____	_____
Job 3 _____	_____	_____
Job 4 _____	_____	_____
Misc Income _____	_____	_____
Bonuses _____	_____	_____
Interest _____	_____	_____
Dividends _____	_____	_____
Rents _____	_____	_____
Alimony _____	_____	_____
Child Support	_____	_____
Unemployment	_____	_____
Social Security	_____	_____
Pensions	_____	_____
Disability Income	_____	_____
Other _____	_____	_____

Total Monthly Income: _____

Total Annual Income: _____

Forms

Vertical Vision

There is hope.

Expenses	Amount	Description/Frequency
Savings:		
Charitable Gifts	_____	_____
Emergency Fund/Savings	_____	_____
College Savings	_____	_____
Retirement Account	_____	_____
Housing:		
First Mortgage	_____	_____
Second Mortgage	_____	_____
Real Estate Taxes	_____	_____
Homeowners Insurance	_____	_____
Repairs/Maintenance	_____	_____
Other _____	_____	_____
Utilities:		
Electricity	_____	_____
Water	_____	_____
Gas/Oil/Propane	_____	_____
Phone	_____	_____
Trash	_____	_____
Cable/Satellite TV	_____	_____
Other Housing _____	_____	_____
Food:		
Groceries	_____	_____
Eating Out	_____	_____

Budgeting Made Easy

Vertical Vision

There is hope.

Transportation:
Car Payment 1 _____ _____ _____

Car Payment 2 _____ _____ _____

Gasoline _____ _____

Repairs and Tires _____ _____

Auto Insurance _____ _____

Registration Fees _____ _____

Auto Replacement _____ _____

Misc. _____ _____

Other _____ _____ _____

Clothing:
Adults _____ _____

Children _____ _____

Medical:
Health Insurance _____ _____

Disability Insurance _____ _____

Doctors _____ _____

Dentist _____ _____

Optometrist _____ _____

Medicine _____ _____

Forms

Vertical Vision

There is hope.

Personal:

Life Insurance	_____	_____
Child Care	_____	_____
Baby Sitter	_____	_____
Toiletries	_____	_____
Cosmetics	_____	_____
Hair Care	_____	_____
Education - Adults	_____	_____
Education – Children	_____	_____
School Supplies	_____	_____
Subscriptions	_____	_____
Organization Dues	_____	_____
Christmas Gifts	_____	_____
Birthday Gifts	_____	_____
Cell Phone 1	_____	_____
Cell Phone 2	_____	_____
Spending Money	_____	_____
Supporting Others	_____	_____
Misc.	_____	_____
Other _____	_____	_____
Other _____	_____	_____
Other _____	_____	_____

web: www.verticalvisionmedia.com

12101 North MacArthur Blvd Box 256
Oklahoma City, Oklahoma 73162

Budgeting Made Easy

Vertical Vision

There is hope.

Recreation:
Entertainment _____ _____

Vacation _____ _____

Other _____ _____

Obligations:
Alimony _____ _____

Child Support _____ _____

Debts:
Credit Card 1 _____ _____ _____

Credit Card 2 _____ _____ _____

Credit Card 3 _____ _____ _____

Credit Card 4 _____ _____ _____

Credit Card 5 _____ _____ _____

Credit Card 6 _____ _____ _____

Store Card 1 _____ _____ _____

Store Card 2 _____ _____ _____

Store Card 3 _____ _____ _____

Student Loan 1 _____ _____

Student Loan 2 _____ _____

Other _____ _____ _____

Other _____ _____ _____

Other _____ _____ _____

Other _____ _____ _____

Forms

Vertical Vision

There is hope.

Total Monthly Expenses _____   _____

Total Monthly Income: _____
Total Monthly Expenses - _____
Difference   = _____

If the amount in difference is a negative number, then you are overspending by this amount. You need to adjust your monthly expenses so that you are no longer overspending.

If the amount in difference is a positive number, congratulations, you are spending less than you make. This money should be used to build an emergency fund, pay down debt, and save for future goals.

web: www.servethroughmedia.com

12101 North MacArthur Blvd Box 266
Oklahoma City, Oklahoma 73162

Budgeting Made Easy

Forms

Debt Pay Down Plan

Instructions:

List each debt from the smallest total debt to the largest total debt. Fill in each blank showing the total amount due, the monthly minimum payment, and the interest rate.

Every month, you will pay only the minimums due on every debt except the first one on the list. The fist debt on the list you will pay the minimum due plus any "extra" money you have. You can use our Monthly income worksheet to calculate your "extra" money.

When you completely pay off a debt, cross it off the list and give yourself a pat on the back for paying off a debt.

You will now work on paying off the next debt. On the next debt you will pay the minimum amount, plus the minimum amount that you were paying to the debts above it (that have now been paid off) on the list, plus any "extra" money you have.

This is commonly referred to as the Debt Snowball. Every time you pay off a debt, the snowball grows larger picking up speed and size to help pay off the next debt. This method of paying off debt is the best method used because it keeps showing progress and helps you stay on track. Other methods that use interest rates and tax burden calculations show little progress and cause most people to give up because they don't see the progress.

Post your Debt Pay Down Plan somewhere will you will constantly see it, like on your refrigerator. This will serve as a constant reminder of your goal to eliminate debt and a constant reminder of the debts you already crossed off the list.

Forms

Vertical Vision

There is hope.

Debt Pay Down Plan

Debt:	Total Debt:	Minimum Payment:	Interest Rate:
_____	_____	_____	_____
_____	_____	_____	_____
_____	_____	_____	_____
_____	_____	_____	_____
_____	_____	_____	_____
_____	_____	_____	_____
_____	_____	_____	_____
_____	_____	_____	_____
_____	_____	_____	_____
_____	_____	_____	_____
_____	_____	_____	_____
_____	_____	_____	_____
_____	_____	_____	_____
_____	_____	_____	_____
_____	_____	_____	_____
_____	_____	_____	_____
_____	_____	_____	_____
_____	_____	_____	_____
_____	_____	_____	_____
_____	_____	_____	_____
_____	_____	_____	_____

web: www.servethroughdebts.com

12101 North MacArthur Blvd Box 256
Oklahoma City, Oklahoma 73162

Budgeting Made Easy

Forms

Pro Rata Plan

Example:

There is hope.

Pro Rata Fair Share Plan

Debt Payment Money: $ 200   Total Debt Payments: 2,000

Debt:	Total Due:	Total Debt Payments: (see above)	Percent of Debt:	Debt Payment Money	Amount I Can Pay Now:
Sears	100 /	2,000	= 5% (.05) x	200	= $10
Bank of America	200 /	2,000	= 10% (.10) x	200	= $20
Discover	200 /	2,000	= 10% (.10) x	200	= $20
Amex	300 /	2,000	= 15% (.15) x	200	= $30
Home Depot	1,200 /	2,000	= 60% (.60) x	200	= $120
	/		=	x	=
	/		=	x	=
	/		=	x	=
	/		=	x	=

Budgeting Made Easy

There is hope.

Pro Rata Fair Share Plan

Debt Payment Money: $_____   **Total Debt: $_____**

Debt:	Total Due:	Total Debt: (see above)		Percent of Debt:	Debt Payment Money		Amount I Can Pay Now:
_____	_____	/ _____	=	_____	x _____	=	_____
_____	_____	/ _____	=	_____	x _____	=	_____
_____	_____	/ _____	=	_____	x _____	=	_____
_____	_____	/ _____	=	_____	x _____	=	_____
_____	_____	/ _____	=	_____	x _____	=	_____
_____	_____	/ _____	=	_____	x _____	=	_____
_____	_____	/ _____	=	_____	x _____	=	_____
_____	_____	/ _____	=	_____	x _____	=	_____
_____	_____	/ _____	=	_____	x _____	=	_____
_____	_____	/ _____	=	_____	x _____	=	_____
_____	_____	/ _____	=	_____	x _____	=	_____
_____	_____	/ _____	=	_____	x _____	=	_____
_____	_____	/ _____	=	_____	x _____	=	_____
_____	_____	/ _____	=	_____	x _____	=	_____
_____	_____	/ _____	=	_____	x _____	=	_____
_____	_____	/ _____	=	_____	x _____	=	_____
_____	_____	/ _____	=	_____	x _____	=	_____

web: www.seethroughmedia.com

12101 North MacArthur Blvd Box 256
Oklahoma City, Oklahoma 73162

Forms

Credit Dispute Letter

Date:

Your Name
Your Address
Your City, State, Zip

Credit Agency Name
Credit Agency Address
Credit Agency City, State, Zip

I am writing to dispute the following information in my file. The items I dispute also are encircled on the attached copy of the report I received.

This item (identify item(s) disputed by name of source, such as creditors or tax court, and identify type of item, such as credit account, judgment, etc.) is (inaccurate or incomplete) because (describe what is inaccurate or incomplete and why). I am requesting that the item be deleted.

Please reinvestigate this (these) matter(s) and (delete or correct) the disputed item(s).

Sincerely,

Your name

Enclosures: (List what you are enclosing)

Budgeting Made Easy

Forms

Budgeting Made Easy

Endnotes:

---

[i] U.S. Bankruptcy Courts—
Business and Nonbusiness Cases Commenced, by Chapter of the Bankruptcy Code,
During the 12-Month Period Ending March 31, 2013 Table F-2

www.ingramcontent.com/pod-product-compliance
Lightning Source LLC
Chambersburg PA
CBHW072222170526
45158CB00002BA/708